LONDON'S PLAXTON PRESIDENT BUSES

DAVID BEDDALL

AMBERLEY

First published 2022

Amberley Publishing
The Hill, Stroud
Gloucestershire, GL5 4EP

www.amberley-books.com

Copyright © David Beddall, 2022

ISBN 978 1 3981 0620 8 (print)
ISBN 978 1 3981 0621 5 (ebook)

British Library Cataloguing in Publication Data.
A catalogue record for this book is available from
the British Library.

Origination by Amberley Publishing.
Printed in the UK.

Introduction

The President was the only low-floor, double-deck model to be produced by Plaxton. The first example was displayed at the 1997 Coach and Bus Expo in Birmingham, later being displayed in London for the first time at Aldgate bus station for three days during May 1998.

The Plaxton President was constructed at the former Northern Counties factory in Wigan. After the collapse of Northern Counties in 1995 the company was purchased by Plaxton. The President replaced the Northern Counties Palatine II model, which had been produced in the mid-1990s.

This new model successfully competed with Alexander's low-floor, double-deck body – the ALX400, which was introduced around the same time. Like the ALX400, the President became available on the Dennis Trident (later the Transbus Trident), the DAF DB250 and the Volvo B7TL. The Trident and B7TL models proved to be popular with a number of London operators, including Go-Ahead London, First London and Metroline. London United, Sovereign and Durham Travel Services (Easylink, later East Thames Buses) favoured the Volvo B7TL model over the others, with Metroline and First London also taking the B7TL into stock. Arriva London naturally favoured the DAF DB250. Other than a small batch delivered to Capital Logistics, Arriva were the only company to take stock of the DB250.

In total, 101 Plaxton President-bodied DAF DB250s, 873 President-bodied Volvo B7TLs and 728 President-bodied Tridents were operated by London operators. After their London careers, the Presidents found themselves cascaded around the UK. The majority of the DAF DB250s from Arriva London were put to use by Arriva's The Original London Sightseeing Tour, replacing the numerous Leyland Olympians in the fleet.

The Presidents began to leave London in 2005 when First London cascaded some of their early Tridents out to First Glasgow. Metroline was the last operator to work the type in large quantities. It was this operator who was the last to withdraw the type from London service. Harrow Weald-based VP614 was the last of the type to be used, being withdrawn on 23 December 2019.

This book is divided into three sections: the Dennis Tridents feature first, as this was the first type to enter service, followed by the DAF DB250 and finally the Volvo B7TL.

The first Plaxton President-bodied Dennis Tridents entered service with Metroline from Holloway garage between March and September 1999, although the first of the batch – TP1 (T101 KLD) – was delivered in September. It is seen loading at Archway bound for nearby Highgate Village. Metroline took stock of 203 shorter TP class Tridents between 1999 and 2003. (Liam Farrer-Beddall)

The original batch of Presidents featured a centre staircase. This can clearly be seen on TP11 (T81 KLD), seen here passing through Victoria station while heading towards Parliament Hill Fields. The main rival of the President was the ALX400, an example of which can be seen following TP11. (Liam Farrer-Beddall)

TP41 (T141 CLO) is another example of the original batch of Tridents taken into stock at Holloway garage. It is seen approaching journey's end on Route 4 (Archway–Waterloo) just before crossing Waterloo Bridge. (Liam Farrer-Beddall)

Seen at the other end of the route, at Archway, is TP50 (V750 HBY). The centre staircase is again seen clearly in this photograph. The Holloway garage codes are also visible next to the running number. (Liam Farrer-Beddall)

The renewal of rolling stock at Holloway led to the cascade of the original TP class out to Potters Bar. It is at Potters Bar garage we find TP54 (V754 HBY), seen still carrying the Holloway garage code. (Liam Farrer-Beddall)

Another photograph taken at Archway, where we find two Plaxton Presidents. TP57 (V757 HBY) is seen operating Route 271 to Highgate Village. A difference in the height of the blue skirt can be seen on the two vehicles. (Liam Farrer-Beddall)

Thirty-three longer TPL class Plaxton President-bodied Dennis Tridents were taken into stock between January and March 2002. They were originally allocated to Harrow Weald for Route 140/N140. These longer examples measured 10.5 m and featured an extra, small window bay just behind the centre exit doors. Only sixty of the longer TPL class were purchased by Metroline. TPL248 (LN51 KYC) is seen inside Potters Bar garage, taken during one of the company's first open days. (Liam Farrer-Beddall)

Metroline's Potters Bar garage operates a handful of non-Transport for London services. For this, the company uses vehicles in a blue, white and red livery known as the Hertfordshire livery. TPL249 (LN51 KYE) partially shows this off, but is also seen carrying an advert for unlimited travel in St Albans. TPL249 is seen passing through Barnet, bound for St Albans on Route 84. (Liam Farrer-Beddall)

North Finchley finds Potters Bar-based TPL253 (LN51 KYJ) on layover. The original smart, red and blue livery applied to Metroline's buses during the 1990s and early 2000s can be seen here. The bus stands at North Finchley near to the bus station. (Liam Farrer-Beddall)

Before major works around Victoria commenced, the streets surrounding the station were used by a number of services as bus stands. This is demonstrated by Metroline's TPL260 (LN51 KYU). It is seen on layover, blinded and ready for its return journey to its home garage at Cricklewood. (David Beddall)

Muswell Hill finds TPL261 (LN51 KYV), seen while allocated to Holloway garage, operating a journey on Route 43 towards Friern Barnet. Muswell Hill is itself a busy intersection for a number of London routes, either passing through or terminating there, including the busy trunk routes 43 and 134. (David Beddall)

Twenty-seven Transbus President-bodied Tridents were taken into stock by Metroline during May 2002, split between Potters Bar and Holloway. The first five (TPL270–274) were allocated to Potters Bar where they were worked on the garage's double-deck routes. TPL274 (LR02 BBE) is captured by the camera having a day out on the 84s (St Albans–New Barnet), on layover on St Peters Street, St Albans. (Liam Farrer-Beddall)

Cricklewood garage provides the backdrop to this photograph of TPL276 (LR02 BBJ). It is seen preparing to embark on its journey to Victoria – contrary to the blind. The replacement of the President, the ADL Enviro 400, can be seen behind TPL276. (Liam Farrer-Beddall)

Marble Arch finds TPL283 (LR02 BBZ) operating a journey on Route 82 towards North Finchley. The additional length of the TPL class can be seen through the addition of the smaller windows behind the staircase, as can be clearly seen here. (Liam Farrer-Beddall)

The southern end of Route 82, Victoria, finds TPL291 (LR02 BCY) having just departed its first stop. The Apollo Theatre can be seen just behind the vehicle. (Liam Farrer-Beddall)

Potters Bar garage finds TPL296 (LR02 BDU) while having a rest, previously operating Route 82. This photograph can now be considered an historic shot as none of the vehicles pictured here are in London service. Prominent Dennis and Plaxton badges can be seen on the front of the vehicle. TPL296 was numerically the last long Trident. (Liam Farrer-Beddall)

TP375 (LR52 KWY) is seen parked on layover at Greenford Broadway while operating Route E2. This was one of a large batch originally allocated to Cricklewood garage for the conversion of numerous double-deck routes operating into central London. (David Beddall)

The front seats of a double-decker can often be a good spot to take photos of buses going in the opposite direction. It is from this vantage point that TP391 (LR52 KXK) is captured travelling to Waterloo, passing Selfridges on Oxford Street. (Liam Farrer-Beddall)

Sister vehicle TP392 (LR52 KXL) is captured the more conventional way while operating Route 32 to Edgware station. It is seen about to turn into Edgware station and is followed by an ADL Enviro 400. (Liam Farrer-Beddall)

TP401 (LR52 KXW) was another of the batch allocated to Cricklewood garage. It is seen about to turn into Buckingham Palace Road to head towards Victoria station to start up a journey on Route 16 towards its home garage. Victoria coach station is just on the left of the photograph. (Liam Farrer-Beddall)

TP407 (LK03 CEX) was new to Metroline's Cricklewood garage in March 2003. It later transferred to Metroline's Hertfordshire outpost, Potters Bar. It is from this garage that Route 217 operated for a number of years before being lost to Sullivan Buses. TP407 is photographed having just left Turnpike Lane station, heading for Waltham Cross. (Liam Farrer-Beddall)

Archway finds Holloway-based TP410 (LK03 CFD), another March 2003 delivery that originally operated from Cricklewood garage. It is seen operating Route 271 to Highgate Village. London's low-floor buses have always carried a small wheelchair logo on the front of the vehicle to denote that they have a low floor. This sign is seen next to the roundel on the front, nearside of the vehicle. (Liam Farrer-Beddall)

The spring of 2003 saw the delivery of ten Transbus President-bodied Transbus Tridents to Holloway garage. It later transferred across to Cricklewood garage, from where Route 189 (Brent Cross–Oxford Circus) operates. TP420 (LK03 GFV) is seen leading a line of Plaxton Presidents on layover at Brent Cross Shopping Centre before heading back into central London. (Liam Farrer-Beddall)

An area not traditionally associated with Metroline is Walthamstow in East London. However, it is at this location that we find TP425 (LK03 GGF), seen operating a rail replacement service for the Victoria Line. Another Metroline President can be viewed in the distance. (Liam Farrer-Beddall)

Sister vehicle TP426 (LK03 CGG) is found loading opposite Wembley Park Underground station while heading for Harrow Weald on Route 182. Originally allocated to Holloway garage where it was used to replace older VPL class Presidents to Edgware, it was later reallocated to Harrow Weald. (Liam Farrer-Beddall)

June 2003 saw the delivery of further Transbus Trident/President vehicles. Allocation of this batch was split between Park Royal and Potters Bar garages. TP444 (LK03 GHB) was one allocated to the latter garage. It is seen passing Edmonton Green bus station while heading towards Chase Farm Hospital. (Liam Farrer-Beddall)

TP448 (LK03 GHH) is another of the June 2003 delivery to be allocated to Potters Bar garage. Although this garage is located in Hertfordshire, they operated into central London on Route 82 (North Finchley–Victoria). A revision of Route 13 in April 2017 saw the withdrawal of the 82. TP448 is seen rounding Marble Arch while heading toward North Finchley. (Liam Farrer-Beddall)

Another view taken passing Edmonton Green bus station. TP457 (LK03 GJG) is the vehicle concerned. It shows off the red and blue livery applied to Metroline vehicles prior to the 100 per cent red rule that was introduced by TfL. (Liam Farrer-Beddall)

Waltham Cross is the most northerly bus station owned by Transport for London. It is at this location where we find Potters Bar-based TP462 (LK03 GJZ). It is seen departing Waltham Cross, heading for Turnpike Lane station, on Route 217. (Liam Farrer-Beddall)

TP1509 (LK03 NKD) was new to First London in April 2003 as TN1278. In June 2013, First sold its London operations, with Metroline and Tower Transit taking over various garages. Metroline took control of Willesden Junction, Greenford, Hayes and Uxbridge garages. The Presidents were renumbered into the Metroline numbering series. TP1509 is seen passing through Greenford Broadway. (Liam Farrer-Beddall)

New to First London in May 2003 as TN1333, TP1530 (LK03 UFM) was allocated to Uxbridge garage and primarily used on Route U4 (Uxbridge–Hayes). TP1530 is photographed passing Hayes and Harlington station in West London, bound for Uxbridge. (Liam Farrer-Beddall)

A trio of Tridents are seen parked at Potters Bar garage. TPL296 (LR02 BDU), TP426 (LK03 CCG) and TP455 (LK03 GHZ) are the vehicles captured on camera in this view. (Liam Farrer-Beddall)

The former First Capital garage at Hackney finds a pair of Plaxton President-bodied Dennis Tridents. TN32804 (T804 LLC) and TNL32899 (V899 HLH) can be viewed in this photograph, along with one of the numerous Marshall Capital-bodied Dennis Dart SLF saloons purchased by First London. (David Beddall)

September 2004 saw a number of buses around London gain a blue-based livery for the 'Back the Bid' campaign, supporting London's application to host the London 2012 Olympic Games. Showing off this livery is First London's Dennis Trident TN32808 (T808 LLC), seen parked in the yard of the former First Capital's Hackney garage. This site now forms part of Olympic Park. (David Beddall)

Thirty-four Plaxton President-bodied Dennis Tridents were taken into stock by First Capital at Dagenham garage for use on routes 1 and 25 over the summer of 1999. TN32873 (T873 KLF) was originally numbered TN873 and was delivered in August. It is seen on layover at Edmonton bus station while operating Route 191. (Liam Farrer-Beddall)

Uxbridge took stock of a number of longer TNL class Tridents between March and April 2000 for use on Route 207. Originally numbered TNL893 (V893 HLH), this 10.47-metre-long Trident can be seen loading at Uxbridge station, about to start a journey on the semi-express service 607 to White City, a route that parallels the 207 between Hayes By-Pass and White City. It is seen wearing its five-digit fleet number, TNL32893. (Liam Farrer-Beddall)

Another of the longer Tridents originally allocated to Uxbridge garage is TNL32896 (V896 HLH). It is seen in pastures new after transfer to Alperton garage. Wembley High Road is the location of this photograph, with TNL32896 seen operating a journey on Route 92 towards Ealing Hospital. (Liam Farrer-Beddall)

Seventeen Plaxton President-bodied Dennis Tridents were taken into stock at Greenford garage during June 2001 for use on the 105/N105 services between Greenford and Heathrow Airport. They did, however, find their way onto other services from Greenford garage, as is demonstrated here. Originally numbered TN993 (Y993 NLP), TN32993 is seen on layover at Ealing Broadway before embarking on a short working on Route E1 back to Greenford Broadway. (David Beddall)

Shepherd's Bush Green finds TN33059 (LN51 GJO) almost at journey's end at White City while operating Route 607 from Uxbridge. This was one of twenty-four Dennis Tridents delivered to First London during December 2001. This sizeable batch was originally delivered to First Capital's Dagenham garage for routes 179 and 365. (Liam Farrer-Beddall)

In addition to the twenty-four shorter Tridents allocated to Dagenham, the garage also took stock of twelve longer Tridents in December 2001. Representing this batch is TNL33078 (LN51 GNJ), originally numbered TNL1078. It is seen passing through Ilford Broadway while operating a journey on Route 179. (Liam Farrer-Beddall)

TNL33091 (LN51 GMY) formed part of a batch of sixteen Plaxton President-bodied Dennis Tridents taken into stock by First London in January 2002. These were again allocated to Dagenham where they were to be used on routes 123 and 252. Canning Town provides the backdrop to 33091, which is seen operating a rail replacement service. (Liam Farrer-Beddall)

TNL33098 (LN51 GOA) is the penultimate member of the batch originally numbered TNL1072–1099, which were first allocated to Dagenham. It is seen while operating from Uxbridge garage on a journey from Uxbridge to White City on the 607. Ealing Broadway is the location of this photograph. (Liam Farrer-Beddall)

TN1113 (LT02 NVX) was one of fifty London buses painted gold in 2002 in celebration of Elizabeth II's Golden Jubilee. It is seen attending the 2002 Showbus rally at the Imperial War Museum, Duxford, while carrying this livery. (Gary Seamarks)

March and April 2002 saw the delivery of seventeen Tridents to Northumberland Park garage for operation on Route 91 (Crouch End–Trafalgar Square). Members of the batch, TN1113–1129, could often be found operating other services from this garage. This is demonstrated here by TN33124 (TN1124, LT02 NVM), which is seen about to cross Waterloo Bridge on Route 341. (Liam Farrer-Beddall)

Eleven longer Tridents were taken into stock at Uxbridge garage during May 2002 to cover additional work on the 207 service. As has already been seen, the 607 also featured members of the batches intended for the route. This is again depicted in this view of TNL33131 (LT02 ZBX), which is seen dropping off passengers at Shepherd's Bush station just before completing the short journey towards White City bus station. (Liam Farrer-Beddall)

TNL33138 (LT02 ZFK) is another member of the eleven extra Tridents purchased to operate Route 207. It is again seen passing through Shepherd's Bush station, about to drop off passengers. The replacement for these vehicles, the Mercedes-Benz Citaro, can just be glimpsed on the right. (Liam Farrer-Beddall)

The West London garage of Hayes, now owned by Metroline, finds TN33159 (LR02 LXU). During its operational years with First London, Hayes garage was used as an operational base for a number of routes, including the 207 during the bendy bus era. It was also used as a storage location of new and decommissioned First London vehicles. (Liam Farrer-Beddall)

The streets surrounding Greenford Broadway are home to a number of bus stands for various routes terminating there. This is demonstrated by TNL33160 (LR02 LXV), which is seen on layover having completed a journey on the E3. The original First London livery can be seen clearly in this photograph. (David Beddall)

Twenty-two Tridents were ordered for delivery to Westbourne Park garage to convert Route 295 to the type. TN33186 (LT52 WVB) was part of this batch but was diverted when new in September 2002 to Alperton to help out there; however, it eventually moved to its intended garage. It is seen travelling down the Strand towards Liverpool Street on Route 23. (Liam Farrer-Beddall)

The introduction of new rolling stock on services in central London often leads to the cascade of older rolling stock out to other garages in London. Originally allocated to Westbourne Park, TN33193 (LT52 XAB) is seen operating from Uxbridge garage. It is seen leaving Uxbridge station, bound for nearby Hayes, on Route U4. It is showing the 100 per cent red livery imposed on London operators by Transport for London. (Liam Farrer-Beddall)

Twenty shorter Tridents were purchased by First London to cover the requirements on Route 414 (Maida Vale–Putney Bridge) when this route was introduced in November 2002. This route originally operated from Westbourne Park garage. TNL33229 (LT52 WXG) is seen off route, being used on rail replacement work, passing through Aldgate. (Liam Farrer-Beddall)

The year 2003 saw the intake of thirty-two Transbus President-bodied Transbus Tridents with First London, split into two batches. Fifteen such vehicles were allocated to Uxbridge garage where they were mainly put to use on local services. TN33333 (LK03 UFM), originally numbered TN1333, is seen passing the entrance to Uxbridge station while operating a journey on Route U4 from Hayes. Uxbridge also sees a handful of non-TfL services pass through, demonstrated by the Carousel Buses Mercedes-Benz Citaro bound for Heathrow Airport in the background. (Liam Farrer-Beddall

The original fifteen Tridents delivered to Uxbridge garage in 2003 arrived during May. TN33337 (LK03 UFS) is another example to represent this batch, seen wearing the 100 per cent red livery. It is seen departing Uxbridge station on Route U4 to Hayes. (Liam Farrer-Beddall)

Go-Ahead London took stock of thirteen Plaxton President-bodied Dennis Tridents in October 2000. Allocated to Stockwell garage, these vehicles were mainly used on Route 88 (Clapham Common–Camden Town). The last of the batch, PDL13 (X613 EGK), is seen passing through Piccadilly Circus heading towards Clapham Common. (David Beddall)

Over the course of March and April 2003 Stockwell took delivery of twenty-three Plaxton President-bodied Transbus Tridents. They displaced PVLs that had been loaned to the garage, these being transferred to New Cross and Peckham. These vehicles were intended to operate Route 133 (Liverpool Street Station–Streatham Hill), but could also be found on other routes. PDL30 (PN03 ULW) is photographed on layover at Tooting Broadway. (David Beddall)

August 2008 saw the extension of Hackney Community Transport's Route 388 from Blackfriars station to Temple, running via Victoria Embankment to its stand in Northumberland Avenue. This extension was partly due to the rebuild of Blackfriars station, which commenced in 2009. To assist the existing fleet a small number of Plaxton President-bodied Dennis Tridents were loaned from Dawson Rentals to Hackney Community Transport over the course of 2010. HTP4 (PN03 UMK) was one such vehicle, originating with Go-Ahead London as their PDL50. (Liam Farrer-Beddall)

The hired Tridents could also be found on other services operated by Hackney Community Transport. This is demonstrated by HTP6 (PN03 ULY), which is seen arriving at Leytonstone on Route W13, traditionally operated by single-decks. Acquired by Hackney Community Transport in October 2010, this vehicle was new to Go-Ahead London as PDL39. (Liam Farrer-Beddall)

EY03FNL was new to Blue Triangle in April 2003 as TL928. In June 2007 it passed to Go-Ahead London when this company acquired the Blue Triangle business. Lasting until March 2009, it then passed to Ensignbus, Purfleet (dealer), and then on to Sullivan Buses, South Mimms. With this operator it was put to use on TfL school services in North London and rail replacement services. TPL928 is found about to cross Putney Bridge while operating a rail replacement service. (Liam Farrer-Beddall)

Tower Transit took stock of three Transbus Trident/Presidents when they acquired the Westbourne Park and Lea Interchange garages of First London in June 2013. Two further examples were acquired by the company in February 2014. TN33197 (LT52 XAH) was one of three acquired in 2013. It is seen operating Route 31 (Camden Town–White City), crossing Kilburn High Road. (Liam Farrer-Beddall)

Big Bus Company took three Transbus President-bodied Transbus Tridents for a two-month loan from Ensignbus, Purfleet. They were put to use as mobile ticket offices and used to promote Big Bus itself. Former Metroline TP413 (LK03 CFG) is seen rounding Trafalgar Square promoting the company. (Liam Farrer-Beddall)

DAF was the second chassis manufacturer to offer a product for the Plaxton President. Again, like with the Alexander ALX400, the DB250LF model was offered. Arriva London was the only major operator to take stock of this combination in London. A small batch of ten similar vehicles were purchased by Capital Logistics during 1999, which were transferred to Arriva London in February 2000. DLP16 (T216 XBV) represents the first batch of DB250s to enter service from Ponders End garage. It is seen approaching journey's end at Turnpike Lane. (David Beddall)

A steady flow of DLP class Presidents were taken into stock by Arriva London North between August and November 2001. These were to be put to use on Route 29 (Wood Green–Trafalgar Square) from Wood Green garage. Route 29 was converted to bendy bus operation in January 2006, at which point the DLPs were reallocated to nearby garages. DLP40 (Y532 UGC) is seen heading towards Enfield Town, passing through Wood Green. (Liam Farrer-Beddall)

Wood Green again provides the backdrop for DLP52 (LJ51 DLX). A delay in the arrival of new vehicles with Arriva London during 2001 led to a number of vehicles being re-registered from their intended registration marks. (Liam Farrer-Beddall)

Turnpike Lane was a good place to see the DAF DB250/Plaxton President combination. DLP57 (LJ51 DKE) is captured running out of service from Enfield. (Liam Farrer-Beddall)

Route 221 (Edgware–Turnpike Lane) gained an allocation of low-floor buses in 2001, although the specified type was the DLA class Alexander ALX400-bodied DAF DB250. DLP70 (LJ51 DLN) is seen working the 221 in place of the normal DLA class. (Liam Farrer-Beddall)

April 2003 saw the conversion of Route 125 (Winchmore Hill–Finchley Central) to low floor when DLPs replaced MCW Metrobuses on the service. DLP80 (LJ51 ORC) is seen passing through Southgate town centre, heading towards Winchmore Hill. (Liam Farrer-Beddall)

Above and below: DLP72 (LJ51 DLV) and DLP73 (LJ51 DLX) are both seen operating Route 329. DLP72 is another DLP captured about to pass through the crossroads at Turnpike Lane. DLP73 is seen close to Ponders End garage, almost at journey's end in Enfield. (Liam Farrer-Beddall)

Route 279 (Manor House–Waltham Cross) was another service to see the operation of DLP class Presidents. DLP90 (LF02 PKJ) is seen about to depart the Edmonton Green stop, bound for Manor House. The DLPs interworked the route with DLA class vehicles. DLP90 was the last of fifteen of the type taken into stock to convert Route 307 to low floor. (Liam Farrer-Beddall)

Enfield finds DLP93 (LF52 URU), one of twenty President-bodied DAF DB250s delivered to Arriva London during December 2002. The Wright Eclipse Gemini-bodied Volvo B7TL VLW class, the main successor to the DLP class, can be seen in the background. (Liam Farrer-Beddall)

DLP102 (LF52 URH) is seen loading at Southgate station while operating Route 125 towards Finchley Central. In this view DLP102 had lost its original Arriva London cow horn livery in favour of the 100 per cent red livery. It also shows off the roundel that had been applied in recent years to London's buses. (Liam Farrer-Beddall)

Another DLP class vehicle captured passing through Enfield town centre is DLP105 (LF52 URL). This vehicle is another example delivered to Arriva London during December 2002. A handful of this batch were originally allocated to Tottenham, although DLP105 was native to Ponders End garage. (Liam Farrer-Beddall)

DLP107 (LF52 UPP) is photographed heading towards Stamford Hill at Tottenham. This part of Tottenham is bus heavy, with Tottenham garage itself being located close to this location. (Liam Farrer-Beddall)

The former Arriva London DLPs were taken into stock by Arriva's The Original London Sightseeing Tour to replace older rolling stock, such as the MCW Metrobuses, one of which is seen here negotiating Marble Arch alongside one of the Presidents. (Liam Farrer-Beddall)

The year 2005 saw the first low-floor buses enter service with Arriva's The Original London Sightseeing Tour (TOLST) operation in the form of Ayats Bravo-bodied Volvo B7Ls. In January 2006 these smart-looking vehicles were joined by the original batch of DLP class Presidents from sister company Arriva London when they became surplus to requirements. These vehicles were renumbered into the DLP200 series, as shown by DLP202 (T202 XBV). It is seen operating Route T1, the longest of the tours, passing through Trafalgar Square. (Liam Farrer-Beddall)

This nearside view of DLP208 (T208 XBV) shows the livery applied to the Arriva TOLST vehicles. It is found travelling down Park Lane. (Liam Farrer-Beddall)

London City Tours got into financial trouble during 2018. The Original London Sightseeing Tour, by this time owned by RATP, took up the slack, honouring tickets purchased from this company. A number of TOLST vehicles received the City Tour London livery. DLP213 (T213 XBV) shows off this livery while stopped at traffic lights in Waterloo. (Liam Farrer-Beddall)

The acquisition of The Original London Sightseeing Tour by French transport group RATP in September 2014 saw the introduction of new livery to the fleet. The company decided to paint the vehicles into the Union flag. DLP248 (Y548 UGC) is seen passing through Trafalgar Square. (Liam Farrer-Beddall)

Above and below: Two views of DLP253 (LJ51 DJY) showing the significant difference between the original livery applied by Arriva TOLST when it was acquired from the main Arriva London fleet in March 2012, and the application of the Union Flag livery. It is seen at Trafalgar Square in the above image, while below we see DLP253 passing Marble Arch. (Liam Farrer Beddall)

DLP259 (LJ51 DKK) joined The Original London Sightseeing Tour fleet in May 2012. It was fitted, like the others, with an electronic destination display. It is seen passing through Trafalgar Square wearing full TOLST livery. (Liam Farrer-Beddall)

Go-Ahead London took stock of the first Plaxton President-bodied Volvo B7TLs in London, the first of which was delivered during March 2000. Allocated class code 'PVL', the first fifty-five of these vehicles were allocated to the London Central's Bexleyheath garage, where they replaced Leyland Titans and Volvo Olympians on routes 89, 229, 401 and 422. These early B7TLs featured a centre staircase, as can be seen here on the first of the type – PVL1 (V301 LGC). It is seen departing Bexleyheath town centre on Route 89, bound for Lewisham. (David Beddall)

PVL16 (V816 KGF) was one of the first Volvo B7TLs to be delivered to London Central, arriving in March 2000. It is seen negotiating the bus stands at Bexleyheath town centre, displaying the original London Central fleet names. It is found operating a journey on Route 401 towards Thamesmead, a service that commenced at Bexleyheath garage. (Liam Farrer-Beddall)

Delivery of the first fifty-five Volvo B7TLs for the Go-Ahead London group took place over the months of March and April 2000. Seen on layover at Bexleyheath is PVL23 (V923 KGF), having completed a journey on the 422 (Bexleyheath–North Greenwich Station). PVL23 was one of thirty-five PVLs to be transferred to sister company Go North East during April and May 2011 after being displaced by newer Volvo B9TLs. (Liam Farrer-Beddall)

London's buses can often be found operating off their normal routes on rail replacement services, taking them to areas of London that they are not traditionally seen. Lewisham is the closest place to central London that vehicles from Bexleyheath garage normally operate. Victoria finds PVL31 (V331 LGC) travelling towards Brixton and covering for the Victoria Line. (Liam Farrer-Beddall)

PVL56 to PVL143 were next to be delivered, shared between Stockwell and Merton garages. PVL57 (W457 WGH) was originally allocated to Stockwell garage for routes 37, 77A and 88. It later moved to Merton before transferring again to Bexleyheath. It is found in Woolwich operating Route 422 towards Bexleyheath. The London General fleet names and Merton (AL) garage codes are still visible on this vehicle. (David Beddall)

During the London 2012 Olympic Games a number of extra buses were drafted in to increase the capacity and frequency on Transport for London (TfL) services in the Stratford area. Demonstrating this is PVL88 (W488 WGH), which by 2012 had transferred to Go-Ahead London's Commercial Services fleet. Note the white band around the centre of the vehicle, which helped to distinguish this fleet from the main TfL fleet. PVL88 is seen bound for Stratford, passing through Bow. (Liam Farrer-Beddall)

It has already been mentioned that Route 88 (Camden Town–Clapham Common) was one of three services that saw London General allocate the Volvo B7TL/Plaxton President combination to in the summer of 2000. PVL93 (W493 WGH) negotiates its way around Trafalgar Square while heading towards Clapham Common. Another Volvo B7TL can be glimpsed in the background, which is carrying the East Lancs Myllennium Vyking body style. (Liam Farrer-Beddall)

The summer of 2000 saw forty-seven Plaxton President-bodied Volvo B7TLs purchased by Go-Ahead London for use from Merton garage, where they were used on routes 44, 77, 270 and 280. PVL108 (W508 WGH) represents this batch after transfer to New Cross garage. It is seen heading towards Catford bus garage on Route 171, passing Waterloo station. (Liam Farrer-Beddall)

Merton's initial allocation of PVL class Presidents were due to convert routes 44, 77, 270 and 280 to the type. In February 2001, Go-Ahead London was successful in winning the tender for Route 118 (Morden–Brixton) from Arriva London. This new service called for twelve double-decks, with the new operator placing PVLs onto the route. The forecourt of Morden Underground station provides a parking area for terminating vehicles, along with a handful of bus stops. PVL124 (W524 WGH) is captured at the Morden terminus. (Liam Farrer-Beddall)

The renewal of rolling stock on London's routes leads to the surplus vehicles either being cascaded to other group companies, sold or put to further use by London companies themselves. A number of PVLs were retained by Go-Ahead London for use in the Commercial Services fleet or as driver training vehicles. PVL141 (W541 WGH) is seen in use as a driver training vehicle entering Tower Hill. (Aethan Blake)

Thirty-five PVL class B7TLs were purchased by the London General operation of Go-Ahead London during October and November 2000, split between Merton and Stockwell garages. PVL150 (X599 EGK) was one of those allocated to Merton garage. It is seen here after transfer to Camberwell, operating a journey on the 68 (Euston–West Norwood), a route that since 2006 has been traditionally operated by WVL class B7TLs. It is captured passing Elephant & Castle Underground station while heading south to West Norwood. (Liam Farrer-Beddall)

PVL152 (X552 EGK) is another of the batch originally allocated to Merton. It is seen on layover outside its home garage. Another PVL can be seen poking its front end out of the garage building. (David Beddall)

As well as operating numerous routes in South West London, Merton garage also operate two services into central London, the 44 and 77. Route 44 travels in from Tooting to Victoria station. PVL161 (X561 EGK) is seen having just departed its central London terminus, heading back to Tooting station. (Liam Farrer-Beddall)

November 2000 saw the arrival of twenty-three PVLs at Stockwell, built to a revised layout. The staircase had been moved behind the driver's cab. PVL171 (X571 EGK) is seen at rest in Bexleyheath town centre after being transferred there in February 2010. (Liam Farrer-Beddall)

The change of layout of the late 2000 delivery of PVLs can be seen much clearer in this view of PVL174 (X574 EGK) taken in Thamesmead. The PVLs replacement can be seen behind – the WVL class Volvo B9TL. (Liam Farrer-Beddall)

Twenty-nine additional PVLs arrived over the course of January and February 2001 to convert routes 343 at New Cross and 118 at Merton. PVL206 (X506 EGK) was part of this batch, and is seen off route in Brixton while operating Route 333 towards Tooting Broadway. (Liam Farrer-Beddall)

In June 2006, Route 77A was renumbered '87' (Aldwych–Wandsworth). At this date, the standard type was the WVL class Wright Eclipse Gemini-bodied Volvo B7TL; however, PVLs could often be found operating the service alongside WVLs. This image shows this, with PVL214 (Y814 TGH) rounding Trafalgar Square, bound for nearby Aldwych. (Liam Farrer-Beddall)

Lewisham finds Commercial Service liveried PVL223 (Y823 TGH) covering for South Eastern trains, with this particular vehicle heading towards Sidcup. Apart from the registration plate, this vehicle is unidentifiable due to the lack of fleet numbers. (Liam Farrer-Beddall)

The Go-Ahead London Commercial Services fleet can often be found outside of the capital on various duties. The company set a small, seasonal operation in the Essex seaside town of Southend-on-Sea, providing a seafront service. PVL224 (Y824 TGH) is captured loading outside Adventure Island on the seafront in this August 2017 view, wearing a revised Commercial Service livery. (Aethan Blake)

Over the course of April and May 2001 forty-two PVLs were taken into stock by London Central's New Cross garage to renew the rolling stock on routes 171 and 172. PVL234 (Y734 TGH) represents this batch and is seen passing Euston station while on rail replacement. (David Beddall)

Another shot of a PVL on a rail replacement service. This time PVL242 (Y742 TGH) is captured by the camera while operating such a service at Gillingham station. Go-Ahead London frequently help out on rail replacements in the Kent area, mainly using their Commercial Service fleet. (David Beddall)

A number of London buses were used to supplement the large-scale transport operation that supported the London 2012 Olympic Games. Go-Ahead London provided a number of PVLs from the Commercial Services fleet. PVL264 (PN02 XBM) is seen exiting the Eaton Manor Transport Hub, which was set up near Lea Interchange garage. Note the blue tape placed on the vehicle for security purposes. (Liam Farrer-Beddall)

Another view of a Commercial Services vehicle operating outside of London. PVL265 (PN02 XBO) is captured by the camera in Eastbourne, operating seasonal service 775. It has completed the journey and is about to park up for the day at the Stagecoach garage in the town, which doubles up as the town's coach park. (Liam Farrer-Beddall)

Forty PVLs arrived at Camberwell between June and August 2002, all intended for use on routes 35 and 40, on which they displaced Volvo Olympians. PVL275 (PJ02 RBF) was one of the June deliveries. The summer of 2006 saw the batch reallocated within Go-Ahead London. PVL275 itself initially moved to Bexleyheath before transferring to New Cross and Peckham. It is seen travelling down Putney High Street while operating from Putney garage on Route 74. It is seen still carrying London Central fleet names and Peckham garage codes. (Liam Farrer-Beddall)

A small number of this batch also transferred across to Sutton garage, from where they operated numerous double-deck routes. PVL283 (PJ02 RCO) is seen in Kingston, starting a journey on Route 213 (Kingston–Sutton, Bushey Road). The 213 terminates to the side of Sutton garage. (Liam Farrer-Beddall)

Sister vehicle PVL284 (PJ02 RCU) operated from Sutton garage between September 2009 and August 2017 before being transferred across to Peckham. March 2018 saw PVL284 transfer to Merton garage. It is photographed at Tooting Broadway, heading towards Putney Bridge. The more subtle Go-Ahead London fleet names can be seen. (Liam Farrer-Beddall)

PVL293 (PJ02 RDY) is seen at the Sutton, Bushey Road, terminus of Route 213. The building in the background is Go-Ahead London's Sutton garage. Other services from Sutton garage also call at the Bushey Road stop, as can be seen by the SOE class single-deck in the background. (Liam Farrer-Beddall)

PVL297 (PJ02 RFF) is seen loading in Sutton while operating Route 154 (West Croydon–Morden). It is seen heading towards Morden. Since 2008, the route had traditionally been operated by the Optare Olympus-bodied ADL Trident DOE class allocated to Sutton. This photograph also shows the fluidity of type allocation to routes. (Liam Farrer-Beddall)

PVL301 (PJ02 RFO) is seen while operating from Camberwell garage. It is seen off its intended routes (35 and 40), operating a journey on the 45 towards Kings Cross, passing through Ludgate Circus. (Liam Farrer-Beddall)

Another view of a Camberwell-based PVL operating Route 45, this time heading towards the southern terminus of Clapham Park. PVL303 (PJ02 RFY) is seen passing Elephant & Castle Underground station. (Liam Farrer-Beddall)

PVL312 (PJ02 TVU) is the last of the forty Plaxton President-bodied Volvo B7TLs allocated to Camberwell for routes 35 and 40 in the summer of 2002. It is seen on layover at Aldgate bus station before heading toward Dulwich Library on Route 40. A comparison can be made in this photograph between the President and its rival, the Alexander ALX400. (David Beddall)

The next thirty PVLs arrived with Go-Ahead London in December 2002, intended for New Cross garage. A delay in the delivery of a sizable batch of WVL class B7TLs to Stockwell saw ten of this batch loaned to that garage, with six others being allocated to Camberwell. PVL317 (PJ52 LVU) was one that was originally allocated to New Cross. It later moved to Camberwell, initially on loan but soon acquired on a permanent basis by that garage. It is captured outside St Pancras International. (Liam Farrer Beddall)

The New Cross batch of PVLs from the 2002 delivery were mainly put to use on Route 321 (New Cross Gate–Foots Cray). PVL323 (PJ52 LWA) is seen passing Lewisham Police Station, operating a short working to Lewisham station on the 321. (Liam Farrer-Beddall)

Heavy snowfall in 2010 saw disruption to the London bus network. PVL328 (PJ52 LWG) is seen passing St Pancras during the rebuild of the station to accommodate Eurostar trains from the Continent. It is seen having just started its journey south to Clapham Park. (Liam Farrer-Beddall)

The PVLs that had originally been intended for New Cross garage but were subsequently reallocated to Peckham seeing service on Route 363 (Crystal Palace–Elephant & Castle). PVL337 (PJ52 LWS) is seen passing through Peckham town centre bound for Crystal Palace. (Liam Farrer-Beddall)

Extra workings take place at weekday peak times on Route 68, these being numbered 'X68'. The X68 runs from Russell Square to West Croydon, serving stops in Holborn, Aldwych and Waterloo before running fast to West Norwood. PVL338 (PJ52 LWT) is seen passing through Waterloo heading towards West Croydon. (Liam Farrer-Beddall)

Lewisham station finds PVL343 (PF52 WPT), new to New Cross garage in March 2003, along with eleven others. It is seen awaiting its return to Foots Cray. (Liam Farrer-Beddall)

PVL345 (PF52 WPV) is another example from the March 2003 delivery. It is also captured passing a busy Lewisham Police Station, this time travelling through to New Cross Gate. (Liam Farrer-Beddall)

Bexleyheath town centre finds PVL362 (PJ53 SOE), one of nine delivered to London Central in January 2004 and allocated to Bexleyheath. It is seen heading towards Lewisham station after travelling to Bexleyheath from Slade Green. The more subtle Go-Ahead London Central fleet names can be seen applied to this vehicle. (Liam Farrer-Beddall)

Nine PVLs arrived at Bexleyheath during January 2004 to replace the remaining Volvo Olympians in operation from the garage. They were also used to cover for the first batch of PVLs that at this time began a refurbishment programme. PVL369 (PJ53 SRO) is seen paused in Charlton while heading towards Bexleyheath on Route 486. (Liam Farrer-Beddall)

Nineteen PVLs were taken into stock at Merton during November 2003 with the intention of upgrading Route 155 with the type. However, as is typical with London operators, these vehicles formed part of a common user pool of vehicles. PVL387 (PJ53 NLD) is seen passing through Tooting Broadway while operating Route 44 to Victoria. (Liam Farrer-Beddall)

Some of the last Plaxton Presidents to be taken into stock by a London operator arrived with Go-Ahead London at New Cross during January 2005. The batch were initially delivered to replace AEC Routemasters on Route 36. PVL395 (LX54 HBB) is seen operating a Victoria Line rail replacement service. It is photographed at Victoria while on layover. (David Beddall)

PVL403 (LX54 GZP) is seen negotiating roadworks having just departed Victoria, bound for Queens Park station. Note the prominent London Central fleet names applied to these vehicles on the side, with a smaller 'Go-Ahead' name above the front wheel arch. (Liam Farrer-Beddall)

An upgrade of the rolling stock used on Route 36 saw the PVLs transfer from New Cross to Merton during 2012 and 2013. PVL404 (LX54 GZR) is seen while operating from its new garage. It is seen heading towards Belmont on Route 280, about to pass Tooting Broadway Underground station. (Liam Farrer-Beddall)

Grosvenor Gardens, Victoria, finds PVL411 (LX54 GZC) heading towards Queens Park station. From this location Route 36 carried on to pass through Hyde Park Corner, Park Lane and Marble Arch before travelling up Edgware Road. (Liam Farrer-Beddall)

Hyde Park Corner provides a lot of interest for enthusiasts and provides a number of angles for you to photograph buses and coaches from. PVL414 (LX54 GZF) is seen rounding Hyde Park Corner, heading west to Queens Park. Another Plaxton President, owned by Metroline, can be seen in the background operating Route 52 to Willesden. (Liam Farrer-Beddall)

London United took stock of a small batch of twenty-six Plaxton President-bodied Volvo B7TLs in 2000. They were allocated to Hounslow garage, mostly for use on the 120, but were also found on other services from the garage. The first of the batch, VP105 (W448 BCW), is seen having just departed Hounslow bus station. (Liam Farrer-Beddall)

Route H32 (Hounslow–Southall Town Hall) was another route that the Presidents could be found operating. VP107 (W451 BCW) is seen on layover at Hounslow bus station, the building behind being Hounslow garage. (Liam Farrer-Beddall)

On the same route we see VP108 (W452 BCW). A contrast between the original livery worn by the VPs, seen above on VP108, can be compared to the 100 per cent livery worn by VP107 in the previous photograph. (Liam Farrer-Beddall)

After the withdrawal of the Presidents from public service, a handful of them were retained by London United for use in their Commercial Service fleet. VP111 (W457 BCW) is seen about to cross Bishopsgate near Liverpool Street station in all-red livery. (Liam Farrer-Beddall)

Twenty Plaxton President-bodied Volvo B7TLs were taken into stock by Durham Travel Services (London Easylink) in January 2001 to operate Route 185 (Lewisham–Victoria). The company fell into financial trouble in 2002, and in August of that year the company was purchased by East Thames Buses, a subsidiary of Transport for London. VP1 (X149 FBB) is seen passing the exit of Victoria bus station just before completing its journey. (Liam Farrer-Beddall)

East Thames Buses was acquired by Go-Ahead London during October 2009 and saw the transfer of nineteen Plaxton President-bodied Volvo B7TLs. Go-Ahead London retained the fleet numbers applied by their former owner, VP1–19. VP6 (X157 FBB) is seen departing Victoria while operating a short working on Route 185 to Bricklayer's Arms, with the full route continuing on to Lewisham. As can be seen, the batch were repainted into the standard Go-Ahead London livery. (Liam Farrer-Beddall)

The other end of the route, Lewisham station, finds a pair of East Thames B7TLs in between duties. VP16 (X168 FBB) and VP13 (X165 FBB) are the vehicles captured. The parking ground at Lewisham station no longer exists. (David Beddall)

October 2013 saw a handful of the VPs retained by Go-Ahead London for use as driver training vehicles. For this they were painted into a white and red livery, as can be seen applied to VP19 (X172 FBB). It is seen parked on the forecourt of Bexleyheath garage. (Liam Farrer-Beddall)

Of the twenty Plaxton President-bodied Volvo B7TLs acquired by East Thames Buses from Durham Travel Services, only nineteen passed on to Go-Ahead London in September 2009. The last example, VP20 (X173 FBB), was retained by Transport for London and converted to partial open-top. It is seen attending the annual London Bus Museum spring gathering at the Brooklands Museum site. (Liam Farrer-Beddall)

Metroline received their first Plaxton President-bodied Volvo B7TL in December 2000 when three examples were delivered to the company. These were of the longer 10.6-metre type and were designated the VPL class code. Between 2000 and 2004, 134 VPLs were taken into stock by Metroline. VPL148 (X648 LLX) was one of the pair delivered to the company in December 2000. It is seen on layover at Edgeware bus station. Twenty-seven were delivered to Holloway for use on Route 134. (Liam Farrer-Beddall)

Metroline has a heavy presence at Brent Cross Shopping Centre, with a number of services operating from Harrow Weald, Edgware and Cricklewood garages. This view of VPL151 (X651 LLX) shows Metroline's presence, with a shorter VP class President-bodied Volvo B7TL behind VPL151, and a DLD class Plaxton Pointer-bodied Dennis Dart SLF at the side. (Liam Farrer-Beddall)

Route 107 (Edgeware–New Barnet) leaves Greater London, running through Borehamwood. VPL157 (X657 LLX) is seen exiting Borehamwood Tesco, bound for New Barnet. (Liam Farrer-Beddall)

Willesden garage finds a pair of Plaxton Presidents having a break from serving the people of London. Closest the camera is VPL175 (Y195 NLK), a 10.4-metre-long B7TL, while a shorter 10-metre-long example, VP521 (LK04 CSV), is behind. The pair are showing the two contrasting liveries worn by Metroline's buses during the 2000s. (Liam Farrer-Beddall)

Willesden garage took stock of the next batch of VPLs for routes 52/N52. VPL179 (Y179 NLK) represents this batch, and is seen heading towards Victoria, passing through Notting Hill Gate. The small window bay in the middle distinguishes this from the shorter, 10-metre-long VP class. (Liam Farrer-Beddall)

Potters Bar garage took stock of the next batch of VPLs, arriving over the summer of 2001. VPL203 (Y203 NLK) was later reallocated to Edgeware garage along with other members of the type. They were mainly used on the 113 (Edgware–Marble Arch). VPL203 is seen heading towards its stand at Marble Arch. (Liam Farrer-Beddall)

Metroline was quite late in taking stock of the shorter Volvo B7TL/President model. The first batch of these 10-metre-long vehicles was delivered over the course of October and November 2002, a couple years later than other London operators. Thirty-one were delivered to Holloway garage for the takeover of Route 24 (Hampstead Heath–Pimlico) in 2002. VP319 (LR52 BLV) is pictured after transfer to Harrow Weald garage, exiting Brent Cross. (Liam Farrer-Beddall)

Wembley High Road finds VP320 (LR52 BLX), one of 171 10-metre-long Plaxton President-bodied Volvo B7TLs to be purchased by Metroline between 2002 and 2004. It is seen heading towards Harrow Weald, Oxhey Lane terminus, on Route 182. (Liam Farrer-Beddall)

The all-over advertisement concept became popular in the 2000s, with a number of different buses advertising West End musicals. VP330 (LR52 BNE) is seen carrying an advertisement for the *Mary Poppins* musical. It is photographed travelling along Oxford Street. (Liam Farrer-Beddall)

A large number of VP class B7TLs were allocated to Harrow Weald garage, operating a number of services centred on the Harrow area of North London. VP335 (LR52 BNN) is seen departing Harrow bus station, heading towards Brent Cross. (Liam Farrer-Beddall)

Wembley Park is almost midway on the 182 service. It is at this location that VP345 (LR52 BOU) is seen loading while heading towards Harrow Weald. It is seen wearing the 100 per cent red livery, along with the original Metroline fleet names. (Liam Farrer-Beddall)

VP346 (LR52 BOV) is seen exiting a wet Brent Cross Shopping Centre heading towards Harrow Weald. Metroline took a large number of Enviro products from Alexander Dennis from 2006, replacing older vehicles in the fleet. Three of the Enviro range can be viewed in the background, along with a Caetano Nimbus-bodied Transbus Dart saloon. (Liam Farrer-Beddall)

VP469 (LK03 GKJ) is seen passing Harrow bus station heading towards Harrow Weald on Route 182. It shows off the 100 per cent red livery. An East Lancs Myllennium-bodied Volvo B7TL can be seen in the background. (Liam Farrer-Beddall)

Willesden garage took stock of a large number of VPs over the course of 2003 and 2004. The first batch arrived in July 2003 and were put to use on the 260. It is on this route we see VP479 (LK03 GLJ) paused at Shepherd's Bush station before completing the short journey to its destination at White City. (Liam Farrer-Beddall)

Seventeen Volvo B7TLs were delivered to Metroline during December 2003 and allocated to Holloway garage, the codes of which can be seen above the running number on the side of VP497 (LK53 LXO). It is seen on layover at Archway. (Liam Farrer-Beddall)

Sixty-nine President-bodied Volvo B7TLs were taken into stock by Metroline over the course of February and March 2004, all allocated to Willesden for routes 6 and 98. VP515 (LK04 CRJ) is seen at Trafalgar Square while operating Route 6. An advertisement for Lycamobile was applied to VP515 in June 2013. (Liam Farrer-Beddall)

A number of routes terminate at the Aldwych, all using bus stands on the inside of the arch. VP518 (LK04 CRZ) is seen parked on the leading stand, with an East Lancs Myllennium-bodied Volvo B7TL parked behind. (Liam Farrer-Beddall)

A large number of Plaxton Presidents were found travelling along Oxford Street, the location of this photograph. These were mainly on routes 6 and 98, as well as the 113 from Edgware garage. VP521 (LK04 CSV) is seen heading towards Aldwych. VP521 will travel down Regent Street, through Piccadilly Circus and Trafalgar Square, before completing its journey to Aldwych along the Strand. Route 6 has since been rerouted from Marble Arch, down Park Lane and Piccadilly to reach the Strand. (Liam Farrer-Beddall)

Above and below: Two photographs taken at Willesden bus garage depicting two of the Plaxton President-bodied Volvo B7TLs. Above we see VP532 (LK04 CUC) and below is VP534 (LK04 CUH). Both routes 6 and 98 terminate at Willesden garage, and use the garage forecourt as a place for layover in between duties. This is the case for both of these vehicles. (Liam Farrer-Beddall)

VP526 (LK04 CTF) is seen about to enter Trafalgar Square after leaving the Strand. It is seen blinded for Willesden bus garage, wearing the all-red livery. An Enviro 400 can be seen in the background. (Liam Farrer-Beddall)

Another view of one of the sixty-nine Presidents taken into stock by Metroline for use on the 6 and 98 taken at Trafalgar Square. A view of Whitehall is just obscured here by the rear end of the coach. To the right of the photograph we see the entrance to The Mall, leading down to Buckingham Palace. (Liam Farrer-Beddall)

The bus stands previously mentioned, located on the Aldwych, finds VP541 (LK04 CVB), seen here in full red and blue Metroline livery. It is seen blinded for its return journey towards Willesden bus garage. The first stop for Route 98 is located on the southern side of the Aldwych. (Liam Farrer-Beddall)

VP568 (LK04 ELJ) was used to promote the City of Westminster College during 2014. June saw this multicoloured advertisement applied to the vehicle. It is seen heading toward Willesden, passing through Marble Arch. (Liam Farrer-Beddall)

Intended for Route 390, VPL583 (LK04 NME) is seen off route on the 43, heading towards London Bridge station. It is captured by the camera passing through Muswell Hill. (David Beddall)

Twenty-three VPL class Volvo B7TLs were purchased by Metroline in July and August 2004 to replace AEC Routemasters on Route 390 (Notting Hill Gate–Archway) in September of the same year. VPL593 (LK04 NNB) is captured by the camera on Oxford Street, followed by a Mercedes-Benz Citaro G bendy bus, the type chosen to replace Routemasters on the 73 a few months previous. (David Beddall)

VPL597 (LK04 NNF) is another of the 390 batch allocated to Holloway garage. A parking ground located just off the main road towards Archway is the location of this vehicle. (Liam Farrer-Beddall)

As is typical with most London types they often stray from their intended service when the need arises. This is the case here with VPL598 (LK04 NNG), seen passing through Archway en route for Friern Barnet on Route 43. Archway is the terminus for one of the few TfL services operated by the Optare Solo, one of which can just be seen emerging from behind VPL598. (Liam Farrer-Beddall)

The final batch of 10-metre-long Transbus President-bodied Volvo B7TLs to enter service with Metroline did so from Harrow Weald garage, with twenty-five being allocated to this garage. They were put to use on a number of the garage's double-deck services. VP607 (LK04 UWN) is seen parked at the entrance to its home garage after operating night service N16. (Liam Farrer-Beddall)

Wembley High Road is the location of this photograph of Harrow Weald-based VP611 (LK04 UWT). This batch was more traditionally found operating Route 140, but often strayed onto other routes from the garage. (Liam Farrer-Beddall)

Metroline became the last operator of the Plaxton President on TfL services. December 2019 saw the final three operating at Willesden withdrawn from service. Harrow Weald garage had one remaining President in service at this time, which became the last of its type. VP614 (LK04 UWW) ran for the last time on 23 December 2019 on Route 140 (Harrow Weald–Heathrow Airport). It is seen out of service on High Road, Harrow Weald. (Aethan Blake)

Brent Cross Shopping Centre finds VP620 (LK04 UXC) about to depart for Harrow Weald. The fleet of Presidents were upgraded to cleaner air emissions, as were a large number of older London buses. This is denoted by the green leaves located just in front of the rear wheel. The Harrow Weald garage code can also be clearly seen underneath the driver's window. (Liam Farrer-Beddall)

VP622 (LK04 UXZ) is seen passing Harrow bus station having just departed from there to complete the final stage of its journey to Harrow Weald, Oxhey Lane. (Liam Farrer-Beddall)

The final nine Transbus President-bodied Volvo B7TLs purchased by Metroline were ordered against an increase in the PVR (peak vehicle requirement) on routes 43 and 134. These additional vehicles arrived in January 2005, with VPL632 (LK54 FWM) representing them. It is seen being used on London 2012 Olympic Games work, about to enter the Eaton Manor Transport Hub, followed by an Enviro 400 from Stagecoach Manchester. As can be seen, no logos were allowed to be carried by buses being used on Olympic work. (Liam Farrer-Beddall)

In April 2002 First London took stock of thirteen Plaxton President-bodied Volvo B7TLs, the first of seventy-six to be taken into stock. These thirteen were originally allocated to the company's Orpington garage, from where they were used on Route 61 (Bromley North–Chislehurst) and were the only 10-metre-long B7TLs to be purchased by First. In 2006 the 61 was lost to Stagecoach, making these B7TLs surplus to requirements at Orpington. They were subsequently reallocated. The first of the batch, VT1100 (LT02 ZCJ), is seen passing through Hyde Park Corner on Route 414 bound for Maida Vale. (Liam Farrer-Beddall)

Kings Cross finds VNL32315 (LK03 NHV), one of twenty-two President-bodied B7TLs taken into stock by First London during May 2003. It is seen wearing the original First London livery, operating Route 476 towards Euston. (Liam Farrer-Beddall)

Thirty-four Transbus President-bodied Volvo B7TLs were taken into stock at Northumberland Park garage in May and June 2003, primarily to replace Dennis Arrows on the 259 and 476. Representing this batch is VNL32316 (LK03 NHX), seen passing through Stamford Hill on Route 67 towards Wood Green. (Liam Farrer-Beddall)

VNL32321 (LK03 NJJ) is another of the thirty-four B7TLs allocated to Northumberland Park garage. It is photographed in a snowy Wood Green on layover after operating Route 67. (Liam Farrer-Beddall)

Go-Ahead London acquired the Northumberland Park garage of First London on 31 March 2012. Included in the sale was six Plaxton President-bodied Dennis Tridents and seventeen Plaxton President-bodied Volvo B7TLs. The Tridents became known as the PDN class, while the B7TLs became the PVN class. Aldgate finds PVN1 (LK03 NHF) operating a rail replacement service. The Presidents were originally used on Route 67 in North London. PVN1 is seen wearing the livery of its former operator. (Liam Farrer-Beddall)

The acquisition of Northumberland Park garage in March 2012 included Route 67 (Aldgate–Wood Green), the route on which the Presidents were employed. PVN3 (LK03 NHP) is seen at Wood Green preparing for its return journey – again wearing First London's livery. The contract for the 67 was lost to Arriva London in April 2013, leading to the withdrawal of the PDN class and the reallocation of the PVNs. As demonstrated in the previous photograph, the first eleven were retained for other duties. PVN12–17 were placed into store and sold. (Liam Farrer-Beddall)

The Elstree Film Studios provides the backdrop to this photograph of VLP20 (PJ53 OUP), captured by the camera at Borehamwood Tesco shortly before terminating in the town centre while operating Route 292. Ten B7TLs were taken into stock in November for Route 292. (Liam Farrer-Beddall)

VLP25 (PJ53 OUY) is seen heading towards Borehamwood, entering Edgware bus station from the opposite direction as the previous photograph. The VLPs were the 10.4-metre-long B7TL/ President combination. The 292 was operated from the London Sovereign garage at Edgware, which was allocated the code 'BT'. (Liam Farrer-Beddall)

London City Tours entered the London sightseeing market during 2014, purchasing a number of former Metroline Plaxton President-bodied Volvo B7TLs from Ensignbus, Purfleet. A red-based livery was worn by these vehicles and featured pictures of London landmarks. Y163 NLK, formerly known as VPL163 with Metroline, is seen sporting this livery while travelling down Victoria Embankment. (Liam Farrer-Beddall)

Trafalgar Square finds former Metroline VPL193 (Y193 NLK) operating with new owner London City Tours. The pictures of the London landmarks mentioned in the last caption can be seen much clearer in this photograph. Y193 NLK was acquired by its new owner in March 2015. (Liam Farrer-Beddall)

Acknowledgements

Firstly, I would like to say a big thank you to my wife Helen for her continuing support throughout this project. My thanks also go to Liam Farrer-Beddall for again allowing me access to his vast collection of London bus photographs, and for proofreading the text. Also, thanks go to Aethan Blake for providing me with photographs and help with those captions. Lastly, my thanks go to Gary Seamarks for providing photographs. Without Liam, Aethan and Gary this book would not have been possible.